W9-AAA-197

I LIKE WEIRD ANIMALS!

Hair-Shooting Tarantulas and Other Weird Spiders

Series Science Consultant:
Dennis L. Claussen, PhD
Professor of Zoology
Miami University
Oxford, OH

Series Literacy Consultant:
Allan A. De Fina, PhD
Dean, College of Education/Professor of Literacy Education
New Jersey City University
Past President of the New Jersey Reading Association

Carmen Bredeson

CONTENTS

WORDS TO KNOW

armor (AR mur)—A covering that protects the body.

breathe (breeth)—To take air into the lungs and let it out again.

burrow (BUH roh)—A hole in the ground where an animal lives.

enemy (EH nuh mee)—An animal that tries to hurt or kill another animal.

hatch (hach)—To break out from an egg.

prey (pray)—An animal that is food for another animal.

sac (sak)—A pouch in an animal or plant.

WEIRD SPIDERS

Spiders live in many places.

They live in trees and grass.

They live under the ground.

Some even live in water or in your house.

Some spiders do strange things.

Others look strange.

Which spider is your favorite?

This spiny spider has pointy armor on its body. It makes it hard for other animals to eat it.

WATER SPIDER

A water spider can spin a house of silk.

The house is UNDER the water in a lake or pond.

The spider traps air bubbles in its hairy legs.

It carries the bubbles to the house.

Now the spider has air to **breathe**.

TRAP-DOOR SPIDER

This spider lines its **burrow** with silk.

Then it cuts a door in the silk.

The spider opens the door.

Its front legs poke out, waiting for a bug to eat.

The spider grabs a bug, then SLAMS the door.

A trap-door spider sticks its legs out of its burrow.

HAPPY FACE SPIDER

A happy face covers the back of these little spiders.

Some faces look like big happy smiles.

Others look like little happy smiles.

The smiley faces may help scare away birds that like to eat spiders.

GOLDENROD CRAB SPIDER

This spider changes color to match a white or yellow flower.

A bee or butterfly lands on the flower.

It does not see the spider.

The spider uses its long front legs to grab the bug to eat.

Warty bird-dropping spider

BIRD-DROPPING SPIDER

ICK. This spider looks like BIRD POOP!

The spider stays very still on a leaf or branch.

Birds think it is just a pile of poop.

The birds do not want to eat poop.

The little spider stays safe.

TARANTULA

Many tarantulas have sharp hairs on their belly.

Here comes an **enemy**.

The tarantula uses its back leg to kick off the sharp hairs. ZING!

The hairs fly through the air.

They stick into the enemy.

OUCH!

Antilles pinktoe tarantula

Baby wolf spiders go for a ride!

WOLF SPIDER

Female wolf spiders carry their big egg **sacs** wherever they go.

When the baby spiders **hatch**, they ride on their mother's body.

Sometimes the tiny spiders even get in her eyes.

RAFT SPIDER

A raft spider can WALK on water.

It spreads its legs over the water and waits.

The hairs on the spider's front legs can tell if a bug or fish is near.

Then the spider zooms across the water to catch its **prey**.

LEARN MORE

Books

Eckart, Edana. *Tarantula*. New York: Children's Press, 2005.

Miller, Jake. *Trap-Door Spiders*. New York: Power Kids Press, 2004.

Parker, Steve. *100 Things You Should Know About Insects and Spiders*. Broomall, Penn.: Mason Crest, 2003.

LEARN MORE

Web Sites

Enchanted Learning
<http://www.enchantedlearning.com/themes/spiders.shtml>
Make spider crafts, color pictures, and label the parts of a spider.

San Diego Zoo
<http://www.sandiegozoo.org/animalbytes/t-spider.html>
See photos and learn fun facts about spiders.

INDEX

For my weird siblings: Ralph, Jack, and Renee

Enslow Elementary, an imprint of Enslow Publishers, Inc.
Enslow Elementary® is a registered trademark of Enslow Publishers, Inc.

Copyright © 2010 by Carmen Bredeson

Library of Congress Cataloging-in-Publication Data

Bredeson, Carmen.
  Hair-Shooting Tarantulas and Other Weird Spiders / Carmen Bredeson.
    p. cm. — (I like weird animals!)
  Summary: "Provides young readers with facts about several strange spiders"—Provided by publisher.
  ISBN-13: 978-0-7660-3127-2
  ISBN-10: 0-7660-3127-6
  1. Spiders—Miscellanea—Juvenile literature. I. Title.
  QL458.B73 2010
  595.4'4—dc22   2008021496

Printed in the United States of America

052010 Lake Book Manufacturing, Inc., Melrose Park, IL

10 9 8 7 6 5 4 3

To Our Readers: We have done our best to make sure all Internet Addresses in this book were active and appropriate when we went to press. However, the author and the publisher have no control over and assume no liability for the material available on those Internet sites or on other Web sites they may link to. Any comments or suggestions can be sent by e-mail to comments@enslow.com or to the address on the back cover.

♺ Enslow Publishers, Inc., is committed to printing our books on recycled paper. The paper in every book contains 10% to 30% post-consumer waste (PCW). The cover board on the outside of each book contains 100% PCW. Our goal is to do our part to help young people and the environment too!

Every effort has been made to locate all copyright holders of material used in this book. If any errors or omissions have occurred, corrections will be made in future editions of this book.

Photo Credits: Andrew Syred/Photo Researchers Inc., p. 16; © Brian Kenney/OSF/Animals Animals, pp. 1, 17; © Darlyne Murawski/National Geographic Stock, p. 10; © Dietmar Nill/Naturepl.com, p. 21; © Hans Christoph Kappel/Naturepl.com, p. 9; Minden Pictures/Getty Images, pp. 2, 5; © Nature's Images/Photo Researchers, Inc., pp. 13, 18; © Nuridsany & Perennou/Photo Researchers, Inc., p. 14; © Premaphotos/Naturepl.com, p. 14.

Cover Photo: © Brian Kenney/OSF/Animals Animals

Note to Parents and Teachers: The *I Like Weird Animals!* series supports the National Science Education Standards for K–4 science. The Words to Know section introduces subject-specific vocabulary words, including pronunciation and definitions. Early readers may need help with these new words.

Enslow Elementary
an imprint of
Enslow Publishers, Inc.
40 Industrial Road
Box 398
Berkeley Heights, NJ 07922
USA
http://www.enslow.com